LOOSESTRIFE

Greg Delanty

Fomite
Burlington, VT

Poems Copyright © by Greg Delanty

All rights reserved. No part of this book may be reproduced in any form or by any means without the prior written consent of the publisher, except in the case of brief quotations used in reviews and certain other noncommercial uses permitted by copyright law.

Publication Date: December 2011

ISBN-13: 978-1-937677-03-9
Library of Congress Control Number: 2011944246

Fomite
58 Peru Street
Burlington, VT 05401
www.fomitepress.com

Cover image: Dance Club in Baden-Baden, Max Beckmann, 1923
bpk, Berlin / Pinakothek der Moderne, Bayerische
Staatsgemaeldesammlungen / Art Resource, NY

Acknowledgements

Agenda, American Scholar, The Atlantic Monthly, The Best Irish Poems of 2007, Green Mountains Review, Literary Imagination, Poetry Ireland Review, Southern Review, The Times Literary Supplement. I'd like to thank my publishers, Carcanet Press, and Louisiana State University Press, for allowing the Fomite Press to reprint a number of these poems from various books of mine, published over the last twenty-five years. The books published by Louisiana State University Press are *Southward, The Blind Stitch* and *The Ship of Birth*. The book from the Oxford *Poets* series of Carcanet Press is *Collected Poems, 1986-2006*. There are also poems here from my next book of poems *The Greek Anthology, Book XVII*.

The translation of the Anglo-Saxon poem 'The Wanderer' is from a book I edited with Michael Matto titled *The Word Exchange, Anglo-Saxon Poems In Translation*, WW Norton & Company, 2010. This translation is a kind of extended epigraph.

I'd also like to thank the Guggenheim Foundation for a Guggenheim Poetry fellowship, which allowed me take time to write a number of the poems, and Saint Michael's College.

The proceeds of this book will be given to the world-wide environmental movement 350.org, founded by Bill McKibben — see www.350.org.

The Hindi word *angrezi* in the poem 'Little India' means 'foreigner'. The Greek word *ostraka* means potshard' and were used as voting tablets.

"One can remain human by *acting as if* humans were, in fact, unequivocally motivated by moral choices, despite all the evidence undermining this presumption. By performing the demanding role of a free moral agent, one can strive to transcend what one knows to be one's natural limitation, and thus one can challenge one's fate."

    -Hunger of the Imagination: Gustaw Herling-Grudziński, Tadeusz Borowski, and the Twentieth Century House of the Dead, *Literary Imagination*

Contents

Proem: The Wanderer i
Preface v
The Skunk Moths 1
Aceldama 2
Loosestrife 3
The New Citizen Army 4
New Ostia 5
The Bombshell 6
Another Empire 7
Backfire 8
A Wake On Lake Champlain 9
The Air Display 10
Names 11
The Alien 12
Unnamable 13
Xmas in America 14
The Shrinking World 15
After Listening to the World News Again 16
The Jar of Effulgence 17
For The Record 19
Us 20
Apology To Crickets 21
In Times of War 22
The Leper and Civil Disobedience 23
Little India 25
White Worry 26
Ostraka 27
Entering the Acropolis 28
In the Country of Liars 29
International Call 30
Oil Spillage 31
The Earth Tearer 32
Mother 33
Patient 38
Family Crest 39
From Woody's Restaurant, Middlebury 40
The Natural World 41
Black Snow 42
Sermon 43
Esperanto 44

Laughter..45
The Caryatids in the Acropolis..46
The New Athena..47
Disarming...48
Wonder of Wonders..49
The First Story...50
Envoi: Monarch Butterfly...53

PROEM

THE WANDERER

The loner holds out for grace
—the Maker's mercy—though full of care
he steers a course, forced to row
the freezing, fierce sea with bare hands,
take the exile's way; fate dictates.
      The earth-stepper spoke, heedful of hardship,
of brutal battle, the death of kith and kin:
      'Often at first lick of light
I lament my sole way—no one left
to open my self up to wholly,
heart and soul. Sure, I know
it's the noble custom for an earl
to bind fast what's in his breast,
hoard inmost thoughts, think what he will.
      The weary mind can't fight fate
nor will grim grit help.
Driven men often harbor
chill dread fast in their chests.
So I, at sea in my angst,
(wretched outcast from my land,
far from kind kindred) brace myself,
having buried my large-hearted lord
years back in black earth. Abject,
I wander winter-weary the icy waves,
longing for lost halls, a helping hand
far or near. Maybe I'll find
one who'd host me in the toasting hall,
who'd comfort me, friendless,

gladly entertain me. Any who attempt it
know what cruel company sorrow can be
for a soul without a single mate;
exile's path holds him, not finished gold;
a frozen heart, not the world's wonders;
he recalls retainers, reaping treasure,
how in youth his lavish liege
feted and feasted him. All is history.
   He who lacks a beloved lord's
counsel knows this story:
whenever sorrow and sleep combine
the wretched recluse often dreams
that he is with his loyal lord.
He clasps and kisses him, lays
his hands and head on those knees, loves
the liberal ruler as in whilom days.
   As soon as the sober man wakes
he sees nothing but fallow furrows;
seabirds paddle and preen feathers;
snow and frost combine forces.
Then his heart weighs even heavier,
sore for the loved lord, sorrow renewed.
He recalls his friends from the past,
gladly greets them, feasts his eyes.
His mates swim in waves of memory.
Those fellows float away in his mind,
barely utter a word. Down again
the man knows he must cast
his harrowed heart over frigid waves.
   It's not hard to guess why in the world
my spirit's in such a stark state

as I consider the lives of those lords,
how they abruptly quit the halls,
those bold young ones. In this way the world,
day after day, fails and falls.
For sure, no man's wise without his share
of winters in this world. He must be patient,
not too keen, not hot tongued,
not easily led, not foolhardy,
not timid, not all gusto, not greedy,
not too cocky till he knows life.
A man should take stock before a vow,
brace himself for action, be mindful
of the mind's twists and turns.

        The wise man knows how ghastly it'll be
when all the world's wealth is wasted
as in many regions on Earth today,
the still-standing walls wind-wracked,
ice-bound; each edifice under snow.
The halls fall, the lords lie low,
no more revels, troops of gallant veterans
lie valiant by the wall. Some fell in battle,
borne away; others borne by vultures
over the ocean; others the hoar wolf
wolfed down; others a noble laid in a cave
—his mien a death mask of grief.
So the Shaper laid the Earth waste,
until, bereft of human life,
the ancient works of giants stand empty.

        Anyone who dwells on these battlements,
ponders each stage of our dark life,
will wisely survey the distant past,

the myriad struggles, and exclaim:
Where's the horse gone? The young bucks? The kind king?
Where's the banquet assembly gone? The merrymaking?
O the glittering glass. O the uniformed man.
O the general's glory. How that time has passed.
Night shrouds all as if nothing ever was.
Now all that is left of those veterans
is a tower wall ringed with serpent devils;
missiles slaughtered those who served,
weapons amassed for mass murder, an incredible end.
        Hurricanes attack the rocky coast.
Snow storms sheet the earth.
Winter's tumult (dark comes then,
nightshadows deepen) drives hailstorms
out of the north to try us sorely.
This earthly realm is fraught.
Fate changes everything under the sun.
Here wealth is brief, friendship brief,
man brief, kinship brief.
All human foundation falls to naught.'
        So spoke the wise man from his heart, musing apart.
Blest is he who holds true. No man should openly bare
his heart's hardships unless he already knows the cure,
that is his great feat. It's well to seek solace
from the Maker, our only security.

PREFACE

I am glad and grateful that this book of overtly political poems is being published by our local Fomite Press. As I have said in a *PN Review* interview, "I believe that poetry makes things happen. W.H. Auden was wrong about poetry making nothing happen—in the most obvious way it gives a job to printers who produced that book with Auden's own poems. A life dedicated to poetry would be empty if I didn't act upon the truth of my poems. For over thirty years I have been what people call 'an activist,' standing in vigils and demonstrations weekly, and taking part in civil disobedience. Art and life are not separate the way people talk of it. I think of Art and life more as a kind of palindrome…."

A number of poems in *Loosestrife* are taken from my *Collected 1986-2006*. Rearranging them in this context highlights them in a more political context, though they should be just as political in the body of the *Collected*, and perhaps truer to the subject of complicity in our lives, since they are less obviously political there. The book *Loosestrife* is derived from another book, *The New Citizen Army*, which has book covers that were pulped from US military uniforms. The poems in this book have been rearranged and new poems have been added.

That Marc Estrin and Donna Bister designed and produced *Loosestrife* is fitting as we three stand with others in a vigil most days at the top of Church Street in Burlington, Vermont. The vigil is a kind of bearing witness to war and destruction of the planet's flora and fauna of our world—as is

Loosestrife. This book also witnesses healthier ways of thinking and being, such as Bill McKibben's 350.org environmental movement (the final poem 'Monarch Butterfly' is especially dedicated to this movement), the tar sand's pipeline protests and the Wall Street Actions.

Greg Delanty, Burlington, Vermont
October 12th, 2011

LOOSESTRIFE

THE SKUNK MOTHS

The family of skunks, their backs to me from our deck,
       are like great black & white caterpillars. I imagine them
the giant larvae of Luna moths or Monarch butterflies,
       their pupae unzipping, tremendous wings unfolding,
fluttering about the summer airways, big as people;
       each revanchist proboscis exacting retribution for those
we've not let flutter down the summers. Imagine
       their eyes, big as cow eyes, gazing, gazing at us.
Imagine the Luna's gossamer tulle wings, the tippets
       brushing us, fanning us tenderly, wrapping us in a veil,
bringing us gently to our knees in a gathering humility,
       brushing aside our mortification, finally at home, natural
in the natural world—their wings our cocoon—becoming
       ourselves, pinioned resplendence, the human mothfly.

ACELDAMA

And Judas cast down the pieces of silver in the temple, and departed....
And the chief priests and elders took counsel, and bought with the pieces
of silver the potter's field, to bury strangers in. Wherefore that field was
called The Field of Blood unto this day.
                                                          Matthew 27:5-8

We drove down what seemed the curve
of the earth, sandwiched in our Ford Anglia.
We were happy as the colors of our beachball,
a careless car full of mirth and singalong songs,
songs that were mostly as sappy
as the soppy tomato sandwiches sprinkled with sand,
which is why they're called sandwiches our father said,
sandwiched himself now in the ground between his mother
and ours. What's the meaning of dead?
Which one of us children asked that as we passed
the spot with the lit steel cross on Carr's Hill,
putting the kibosh on the next song,
our mother about to break into *Beautiful City*?
She crossed herself, saying that's the place they bury
those whose lives somehow went wrong, betrayed
in one way or other, without a song to their names,
or a name, everyone together
and alone without a headstone.
The crepuscular loneliness of the field
shrouded our bright time. Our world,
the city below, shimmered like the silver pieces
scattered on the dark floor of the temple.

LOOSESTRIFE

You have become your name, loosestrife,
          spurting up out of ballast,
a cure brought across the deep
          to treat wounds, soothe trouble.
There have been others like you, the rhododendron,
          the cattails that you in turn overrun.
Voices praise your magenta spread, your ability
          to propagate by seed, by stem, by root
and how you adjust to light, to soil, spreading
          your glory across the earth even as you kill
by boat, by air, by land all before you: the hardy iris,
          the rare orchids, the spawning ground of fish.
You'll overtake the earth and destroy even yourself.
          Ah, our loosestrife, purple plague, beautiful us.

THE NEW CITIZEN ARMY

Today, as every day, you rise up, don your suit,
      denims, dress—whatever fatigues
society rigs you out in. You'll be one among
      minions under orders.
You'll not think of it like this, you'll not
      think once. You will breakfast,
hardly aware that long ago you were drafted,
      a soldier in the New Citizen Army.
This is as it should be; all regulars must be
      mindless in the execution of duty.
You'll drive to work: the office, the hospital,
      the university—wherever you make your living.
All day you will make your dying, a good tax payer.
      After you arrive home you settle back
on the couch, surf the news, the bodies laid out in neat rows,
      men, women, children, parents weeping.
The daily massacre. You have obeyed the command.
      You think nothing of it. You've played your part.
You are the good citizen. Sit back. Relax.

NEW OSTIA

The red glow of the burning city towered into the sky.
The fetus of terror stirred in us. To witness people in flames
leap from windows, call out. Too much.
The old world brought down around our heads.
The aftermath a seething bewilderment.
Tribunes fan the sparks of public anxiety
into panic, dispatch soldiers to ports, stations,
set up roadblocks, search for weapons. Rumors
of another attack. Opposition cowed by accusations
of being soft, unpatriotic. Special measures called for.
A supreme commander set up
to combat threats, terrorist legions.
Powers ceded to our Pompey Magnus
and his cronies, lining their already lined pockets.

THE BOMBSHELL

> Helen: I *never went to Troy; that was a phantom.*
> Euripides, *Helen*

Those within the inner circle knew the story. Even sane,
    family-man Odysseas toed the line after his ruse to dodge
the draft—casting salt for seed, feigning madness—was exposed.
    He shied from leading his men on another assault
to satisfy old brutal ways for the sake of a bombshell.
    Menelaus and the general assembly pumped up the *demos*,
the statesmen preying on their sense of impotence.
    Many declared the gods decreed this war to lighten
Gaia's burden, the weight of ever-increasing humans.
    A whole nation played its part, converting a lie into truth.
Blind Homer played his harp to that fabricated story.
    The phantom that launched a thousand missiles.

        From *The Greek Anthology, Book XVII*
        Danichorus

ANOTHER EMPIRE

In notes to an old Greek poem, the Seleucid Empire is mentioned.
    An empire that was hot on the tongues of its denizens.
Whose fame spread thousands of leagues. Whom folk feared
    and bowed to. All hailed Emperor Hegorgebus,
who, according to the notes, was thought of in later times
    —in the cold horology of the universe, which is quicker than soon—
as a short-sighted, perverse numbskull under
    the thumb of every consul, praetor, general, and goon
in the agora, breaking the coffers, squandering revenue
    on the military while folk starved, the infirm left without care.
Still the *demos* went on glorifying him, their imperial buffoon.

BACKFIRE

You recall how fireworks were invented
to ward off evil, as they rise high
above the Milky Way of Manhattan.

They form into blue, red & white stars
floating in brief constellations,
then scatter like blown dandelions.

Loudspeakers welcome back soldiers
who plug their gas pump salutes
to their foreheads as generals cruise by.

Victory dismisses all who died.
Fireworks turn into flares for help
amid the bustle & boom of bombardment.

One blossoms into a weeping willow and hangs
above skyscrapers rising like tombstones.

A WAKE ON LAKE CHAMPLAIN

As an F-16 unzips the sky
a white-sailed yacht races in
like a surrendering rider
from the plain of the lake and a boy
conjures doves with a piece of cake.

Gas pumps plug their fingers in their ears.
You can hardly hear a child start to cry.
Her father fails to rock her still.
Afterwards he remarks, "This jet guards
Plattsburgh Nuclear Base, or is on border drill."

Now she's mesmerized by a duck & drake
teaching oblivious fledglings
how to play follow-the-leader.
A peace sign spreads in their wake.

THE AIR DISPLAY

Squadrons of geese fall-fly south, moving in
        and out of rank,
honking simply to stay together and to swap
        leader.
The teachers urge the children to look at fighter
        jets, the Thunderbirds,
a name taken from the great Indian bird, but
        nothing is said of that provenance.
The new god rips open the tepee vault of the sky
        above our schools and homes.
No one points out the caret of geese inserting
        themselves peacefully on the day,
or mentions what exactly the Thunderbirds, awesome
        and all as they are, mean to insert.
The geese unravel their chevron ranks, their echelon
        formation and, as if in civil disobedience,
reform again, but this time into a child's copybook
        correct sign.

NAMES

Soldiers carve their names
      on slingstones: Gregory, Hipponik, Dan;
or words like *Ouch*, *You're Dead*, or *This Maims*,
      precursors of bombs named *Little Boy* or *Fat Man*.

                From *The Greek Anthology, Book XVII*
                            Cassandra

THE ALIEN

I'm back again scrutinizing the Milky Way
        of your ultrasound, scanning the dark
                matter, the nothingness, that now the heads say
        is chockablock with quarks & squarks,
gravitons & gravitini, photons & photinos. Our sprout,

who art there inside the spacecraft
        of your ma, the time capsule of this printout,
                hurling & whirling towards us, it's all daft
        on this earth. Our alien who art in the heavens,
our Martian, our little green man, we're anxious

to make contact, to ask questions
        about the heavendom you hail from, to discuss
                the whole shebang of the beginning & end,
        the pre-big bang untime before you forget the why
and lie of thy first place. And, our friend,

to say Welcome, that we mean no harm, we'd die
        for you even, that we pray you're not here
                to subdue us, that we'd put away
        our ray guns, missiles, attitude and share
our world with you, little big head, if only you stay.

UNNAMABLE

More and more we sense it, the old looming terror
children wake out of, sobbing, mumbling
about being adrift in an ocean
of waves, no one able to see the other
in the daymare breaking over our heads,
the hoar breakers erasing our cries, each head
bobbing foolishly, gasping *save us, save us.*

XMAS IN AMERICA

We sit under the conspiratorial winking lights of the tree;
the gifts strewn open, chosen toys already
abandoned by the children running
amid the computer games, superheroes
saving the world, the knights
wielding swords, the jigsaw
of a fire brigade rushing to an explosion.
The grown-ups lounge, stuffed as the basted bird,
bushed from so much bounty and the kids' questions, even
as we know the children light up the house. A regular scene
on this holiday celebrating our childhood's infant god,
the one we sought to emulate, the one we believed in
as our children believe in Santa, while in truth
all we are certain of now
is that, even as we speak, our legions
are off again slaughtering innocents.
The angels harp on above the snow.

THE SHRINKING WORLD
to Mary & Niall on Catherine's first summer

Reading how the European long-tailed tit
builds a perfect domed nest, gathering lichen
for camouflage, feathers to line it
and cobwebs as binding so the nest can

stretch while chicks grow, I thought of you
rushing to crying Catherine, as if her mouth shone
like those of finchlings guiding parents through
darkness. If only chainsaw-armed men,

felling whole forests by the minute,
could have seen you hover around your fledgling,
they would have immediately cut
engines and listened to your lullabying.

But their lumbering motors drone on
in the distance and perhaps approach us.
And what about all those other Catherines,
imperial woodpeckers & birds of paradise?

I sing now like the North American brown thrasher,
who at one point in its song orchestrates
four different notes: one grieves, another
frets, a third prays, but a fourth celebrates.

AFTER LISTENING TO THE WORLD NEWS AGAIN

So, these days one is dimly consoled with the thought
Hell, even the sun will eventually come to naught.

THE JAR OF EFFULGENCE

Driving in brumal, bucolic Vermont I take a wrong
        turn, preoccupied with the radio news:
climate change, war, famine, the whole ding-dong;
          how we must choose
                as the fumes in the rear view mirror are lowlit
                    by the cold, contributing our own wee bit.

The snow glistens, calling to mind the jar
        of effulgence shattering not just over
              this snowland, but over
        the chrome of a passing car,
        the farmyard's heap of manure,
even the silk-lined jackets
        of the prating Suits
        stalking the hallways
        of the Night House, hoarding the shards of light
        in underground shelters out of sight,
lying now through the din of the airways.

                *

Now relax,
we must not let their dark
shroud our lightning-bug existence,
rob us of our modicum of pax,
our birthright spark,
the litscape heliographing,
the light within responding.

I locate myself again, spotting
Camel's Hump slouching
through this white country.
The seeds, shards, sparks of effulgence
shimmer over all and sundry.

FOR THE RECORD

Today on Mallet's Bay Avenue I am undone
    by the redivivus of wonder
and not simply by the winter-blade sun
    stirring up the snow's phosphorescence, the under-
iridescence of a pigeon's neck, the jaguar
    in the guise of the svelte street cat.
                                Not simply these,
but the exhaust fuming from a passing car,
    made all the more visible by the freeze
of air, the cumulus of stacks of smoke
    billowing heavenward from McNeil's Generator
and the jet drawing a line of coke
    behind it on the sky's blue counter.
Yes, these are not breath or cloud or anything
    to be high on; they are undoing our skies:
the car we drive, the coffee pot plugged in each morning
    and so on and so forth, but it's nothing but lies
not to reiterate how we somehow manage mostly
    to live together—confused only by ourselves, our ghostly
genes of fear and survival, too quick to be undone
    by our invention—mad to be under the sun.

US

The snow cap of Mount Discovery is like a white hanky,
    the knots tied in four corners on the shiny dome
of a bald man at a blistering All Ireland final.
    No one here knows what hurling is. A game played by the gods
when they deign to come down and enter the human body.
    Ares, that most unpopular of commanders in chief
even among his peers, has made this country his own.
    Two fighter jets on display scissor the sky's blue cloth
to shreds. They fly above our house in pastoral Vermont.
    People nearby cheer. We are far from home.

APOLOGY TO CRICKETS

When the squadrons of night-dropped parachutists
        on D-Day were scattered far and wide
        across the occupied French countryside,
finding themselves suddenly alone in forests,
        swamps and fields swarming with the Hun,
        they had these thingamajig hand crickets,
clickers you get in Christmas stockings.
        Searching in the dark to hook up with their own,
        they'd cricket code clickclack clickclack
hearing a rustle of movement, footsteps approaching,
        waiting for the answering cricket greeting.
        Tonight, little cricket, unable to hack
news of another war, I came out to our garden
        and had nothing, nothing to cricket-call you back.

IN TIMES OF WAR
(while reading W.B. Yeats and Patrick Kavanagh)

So, the monocled poet delights in the two Chinamen
seated there on the cracked, lofty lapis-blue slopes
under snow drops of cherryblossom. Their serving man
caresses plaintive strings as the brace of wise myopes
in the cute little halfway house, sipping green tea,
stare on all the tragic scene; their ancient eyes glitter gay.
Over them flies the spindly-legged bird, Longevity,
croaking in the mind's ear all will be 'Okay, Okay.'
Elsewhere, a bit along the rocky slope and of a par,
another poet eulogizes geese flying in fair formation
to Inchicore, how their wings will out-wing the war.
Oh, my two poets I steer by, I know my station,
but what of the mother stooped over her child,
the wild pen over the limp cygnet, the pen defiled?

THE LEPER AND CIVIL DISOBEDIENCE
However, Lommán, a very arrogant leper, at the devil's instigation, was for refusing Bridget's food as usual unless Bridget gave him the spear of the aforesaid king who had gone home early that morning.... Then Saint Bridget and everybody asked him to eat but to no avail. Bridget also refused to take food until the high-handed leper ate.
Vita Prima Sanctae Brigitae

Would I were that pain in the ass, incorrigible leper
egged on, they say, by the devil, to test Saint Bridget.
She couldn't be seen to turn this sorry beggar away.
He refused a morsel. In accordance with etiquette,
no one could touch a crumb. You can imagine the curses
of diplomats, wives, officers, back-stabbers, holy men
round the hobnobbing table. Bridget, a trick up
her saint's sleeve, ordered riders gallop after the king,
casting a spell that as much as the king and the army
seemed to ride, they'd not journey beyond the gates,
towing the paraded weaponry the saint blessed earlier.
The messengers, surprised to reach the troops so soon,
related the saint's request, whereby his majesty declared:
'If Bridget were to ask for all our arms, we'd obey.'
The couriers returned, the curses hardly uttered.
Everyone tucked into piping-hot grub, cold-shouldering
Lommán as poetasters read ass-licking rhymes and fools
flattered the notables, the powers that be, with mock jokes.
All considered themselves noble for joshing king,
country and themselves, laughing off discomfort.
As usual actors & singers elbowed each other for the limelight.
Town criers chronicled the event, who wore what and so on.

The king riding off smirked to himself,
dying to test his stockpile of new model spears.
Bridget, playing hostess, wore a forlorn smile, avoiding
the leper's eyes, with his loathsome head in the clouds.
Lommán, feeling a clown, snickers aimed his way,
suppressed a frown, focused on how many mouths
the spear would feed when melted down.

LITTLE INDIA

The frazzled stationmaster in his shabby excuse
for a uniform, shooing away hoi polloi, is surely
a vestige of the Raj who willed this wonder,
coupled with its compartments of class, a system
that's peanuts compared to the native one of caste,
as impossible to grasp as the rupee notes are
for the begging child with stumped hands. Leper,
the poor foreigner who throws the pittance at your feet
is too repelled to risk brushing you, even as chagrin
flushes his face. He muses how you can't even sew
for chainstores on his side of the crooked globe
and brushes such thoughts under the carpet
of his scruples. Child, it's true, I'm the stumped
angrezi who cast the sorry note and forgot you.

WHITE WORRY

He mentioned his box of white noise, how
      he turns on this constant low-level static
to drown out local fighter jets on manoeuvre; the news
      channel permanently on next door; the snarl
of chainsaws devouring the sometime forest
      now become a wood, closing on our back gardens;
the siren and hooting street traffic; all the rest
      of the relentless, varying normal din.
At first, I thought how superfluous, how modern
      such contraptions are, but who am I to talk?
Look how I rely on low-level worries: the phone bill,
      a snub, something I ought to have said—
all my precious white noise switched habitually on,
      the reliable buzz in my head shrouding daily black noise.

OSTRAKA

The eight winds blow,
an earthquake shakes Mount Olympus, cholera
ravages the states, drought everywhere, the mysterious
death of bees throughout the country,
the flowers and crops die, the daily
slaughtering of innocents,
                            and all we do is debate
in the assembly, cast *ostraka*—shards of democracy—
regarding our ships, the color of their sails.

                From *The Greek Anthology, Book XVII*
                Danichorus

ENTERING THE ACROPOLIS

In the temple of Athena Nike, the goddess smiles smugly
    down on the daily tourists in their comfortable Nikes.
She has won again. Not all victory is a matter of war. Complicity
    is the deity hardly anyone sees.

IN THE COUNTRY OF LIARS

Even now you should not believe me.

     I lie my private snow-white lies,
concocted excuses for being late,
        harmless fibs to evade a row.
Why make anyone cry?

     I lie my public lies, a citizen
voting for demagogues, a taxpayer
        dropping the exploding lies
of democracy on unseen people.

     A lie shared is a lie
made truth; easier to excuse
        the black lie, gray lie, blue lie,
purple lie, yellow lie, the blood-red lie.

INTERNATIONAL CALL

A hand holds a receiver out a top-storey window
in a darkening city. The phone is the old,
black heavy type. From outside
what can we make of such an event?
The hand, which seems to be a woman's,
holds the phone away from her lover, refusing
to let him answer his high-powered business call.
More likely a mother has got one more
sky-high bill and in a tantrum warns
her phone-happy son she'll toss the contraption.
A demented widow, having cracked the number
to the afterlife, holds the receiver out
for the ghost of her lately deceased husband.
He's weary of heaven and wants to hear dusk birds,
particularly the excited choir of city starlings.
It's always dusk now, but the receiver isn't held out
to listen to the birds of the Earth from Heaven.
It's the black ear and mouth in the hand of a woman
as she asks her emigrated sisters and brothers
in a distant country if they can hear the strafing,
and those muffled thuds, how the last thud
made nothing of the hospital where they were slapped
into life. The hand withdraws. The window bangs closed.
The city is shut out. Inside now, the replaced phone
represses a moan. Its ear to the cradle
listens for something approaching from far off.

OIL SPILLAGE

A high-diving gannet opens any point
in the water and a circle radiates out.
Every point is the centre.

Tern scissor the gauze of the heat haze,
snipping the air from Africa, nest
under the sky's sunset fuchsia blaze.

Kids cart a dinghy overhead,
reverse from a crab retreating from them
as if the film was held and run backward.

Bull Rock seems ready to charge out
to sea head down, away from danger
rather than on the attack.

None can escape the dark spreading here.

THE EARTH TEARER

It takes Erysichthon to get under the skin of Demeter,
axing trees of the sacred grove to construct a compound
replete with hobnobbing halls, chambers, spas, seraglio.
Even after the blade bites, bark-blood spurting upon
the earth and a green voice warns him off, he hacks on.
Though for sure, this mortal and his minions cleave limb
after limb as a way of normalising plunder,
slashing into bloody oblivion. Dryads broadcast.
Birds scatter. Animalcules and larger creatures cry.
Unseen denizens of purlieus are gone for ever;
cures maybe even for Erysichthon's purblind sight.

Demeter swings into action, dispatching green heralds,
tendril pursuivants to the ends of the earth, orders Famine
to plant a hunger in this noble that grows the more he devours
till nothing's left to procure food but trade his own offspring—
"our legacy" he once called her. What could the child do
but shape-change, sell herself to stay with her father?
Every mouthful increases appetite till he has nothing
to turn on but his own body, the manducation of his own flesh,
biting into the demon of famine swelling within, his stomach
like a starving child's belly, pregnant with hunger. You can
feel the mandibles dissolve round their own dissolving flesh.

MOTHER

At what moment Mort entered the molecules
and triggered fanatic cells to race
ahead at the speed of night, breaking rules,
overwhelming regular cell pace.
surprising the constitution,
we'll never know; whether you were making dinner,
on the bus down town, fixing your hair,
washing dishes, whatever minor
essential chore you tackled with such care.
Nor, can we know why Mort chose
to show up—our mother, our world, our cosmology,
our Blarney Street Gaia, our Dana—just below
the first sphere where you lugged us furled,
curled and kicking into this world.

What to do, but believe the white-coated men, ma,
explorers of your innards, focusing a wee telescope,
on hearing of something called haematuria,
into your system, our worldscope.

*

Pre-empt the very thought
    we have Mr. Mort
        for life-long company,
the first man himself, the Commander-in-Chief we ought
    keep in mind daily, dispatching his army,
        swarming the appalled cells one and all,
storming the good and innocent. What gall.

Our world's under general anaesethetic.
The doctor cuts the first nick.

Quick, cut out the covert platoon,
        cauterise bleeding cells,
        and not a fraction too soon.
              Are they ringing knells?
              Cut and lay them out in a bloody row,
           then suture with simple catgut. Sew
and pray to your God they don't regrow.

             *

Then the suspense, the meaning of hope,
        the not-a-word-time, the learning-to-cope,
            the thinking-the-best,
the worst forgotten in these testing times, each test
        showing up okay,
           negative is the word they say.
How positive can negative be? Listen. Mort knocks.
The chap with a measured box.

             *

No further symptoms,
no blood in the urine,
all your atoms
are just fine.
We should all know such days each day:
        the fridge hums,
           the kettle on the boil calls *cha*,

clothes on the line
wave "Top of the morning, Ma."
A shirt and a blouse link arms.
"The drying is good today
and not a sign
of rain," you say.
The clock strikes a Saturday morning nine.
All the rooftops in our window shine,
heliographing you're fine, you're fine.

*

Brother Doctor wants to talk to us alone.
Yes, it's confirmed. It's a relapse alright.
The word *relapse* is a phone
      ringing in the middle of the night.

*

The destructive cells concealed in your bowels, head
    out undercover
        into the flow of your blood, gather
in the roots of each alveoli, spread,
      undo your parenchyma,
      undo the tree of your lungs, ma.

*

I switch on the daily news to see what's old.
Mayhem and Mort are general.
It seems the whole show is terminal.

What could we do, all told?

*

Nothing else to be done, we said.
Even as we consult, the dire cells spread.
So Commander Cisplatin and Captain Taxol
      are trooped out to give that evil
           shower a taste of their own medicine,
          violence answering violence.
We stick to routine,
even joke. You ask for silence.
You say, "Now please, no fuss.
We, loves, are a credit to us."

*

Now your spirits are up.
You request a cup
of tea—no sugar, just a drop
of milk. You sit and you sup.
You make ready again for hope,
tiresome hope.

*

Our Gaia comes apart.
Turn off the news. Have a heart.
How the world wags. Metastases overtakes
her carcass, causing paralysis, headaches.
For earth's sakes.

All you can do now is vaguely shake your head.
The black-suited cells have nowhere else to spread.

PATIENT

The snow has melted clean off the mountain.
        It's winter still. Yet another indication that Gaia
is in trouble, that things aren't sound.
        The rocky mountain top shines
like the bald head of a woman after chemo
        who wills herself out of her hospital bed
to take in the trees, the squirrels, the commotion
        in the town, sip a beer in a dive. She smiles
to the child staring at her shining head, wishing
        it didn't take all this dying to love life.

FAMILY CREST

The two swordfish in the market are gawked at by all
    who pass. Parents coax wide-eyed children up to ogle.
One grinning family has a photograph taken alongside.
    Picture these noble knights of the sea being caught,
their bodies, great muscles, writhing on the deck.
    The fish could be the heraldic sword-crossed emblem
of a family coat of arms, but their great lances
    are hacked off. All they could emblazon now
is the family Homo sapiens.

FROM WOODY'S RESTAURANT, MIDDLEBURY

Today, noon, a young macho friendly waiter and three diners,
    business types—two males, one female—
are in a quandary about the name of the duck paddling
    Otter Creek,
the duck being brown, but too large to be a female mallard.
    They really
want to know, and I'm the human-watcher behind the nook
    of my table,
camouflaged by my stillness and nonchalant plumage.
    They really want to know.
This sighting I record in the back of my *Field Guide to People*.

THE NATURAL WORLD

The bead-cold eyes of the Great Blue Heron,
    that should be called the Great Grey,
        spot a shiny sliver
looming beneath the water. The silverling fish
    snatches the gnats, links in the great grey chain
        —winged lightlings, gossamer light greylings.
The fish is about to forget itself
        and become the heron,
    the heron being what's called cruel and selfish too,
    but that's natural, grey-winged necessity.
The heron homes-in across the water; the water
    that's as grey as the heron, fish, rocks, day
        and the background glimmering city—
            habitat of the laughing species.
Now it's time to praise the Great Grey.

BLACK SNOW

David points at the two-day snow along Broadway,
      not the natural jaundiced yellow of melting slush,
but bunkers of fallen smog-snow.
      He remarks, "That's what we breathe in every day",
reminding me of how the nuns described the soul
      as a flake of snow and every trespass soot-darkens
that whiteness of whiteness. Ah, the soul of the world
      is made manifest to us today on Broadway and 82nd,
a fuming black exhausted snow-soul, woebegone
      as a bewildered oil-slick bird unable to fly.

SERMON

... we have a savior who has been tempted in every way, just as we are
—yet is without sin.
     Hebrews 4:15

  These days the Savior could not come back
to live sinless amongst us, the matrix beneath the surface
  of daily existence being sewn so intricately
by that crafty angel, tireless Complicity.
  God's temples are heated by oil secured at the expense
of slaughter. The pillows He'd lie on are the down
  of the bird that saved Noah. Even a sackcloth would likely
have molecules of blood in its stitches.
  He couldn't drop down, mosey
around town, take in His handy work: trees rising up
  from concrete, the hubbub of folk about their business,
a passing girl who reminds Him of Magdalene, the smell
  of coffee. How He envies the creature
created in His own image. How He longs to become His image.
  How He pines for this earth. How absurd
the old God feels now. Our Image. Pray for Him.

       From *The Greek Anthology, Book XVII*
       Simeon the Second

ESPERANTO

This morning the waiter in a dingy cafe
      was baffled by my attempt at his language.
Everyone chimed in to translate, all strangers.
      The waiter got it, smiled
and everyone smiled. For a moment it was as if
      a great problem was solved, as if each registered
the answer we forgot we knew, the froth
      of goodwill bubbling up like cappuccino.

LAUGHTER

On Centre Street, Skala, schoolchildren wave flags,
      commemorating another military victory.
Ares smiles smugly on his infants.
      Three old women chat nine to a baker's dozen
outside the laundromat. I haven't a clue about what
      they say, but it's mirthful. The woman
without spectacles breaks
      into laughter, bends over in stitches
with a heartiness I haven't heard for ages
      at whatever the others say.
They've taken everything from life, wear black
      for all the reasons women wear black.
They've outshone even their own god,
      the orthodox God that never laughed.
May the memory of these women, the three graces,
      be with me now and in the hours of our blackness.

THE CARYATIDS IN THE ACROPOLIS

So when the ruling, puffed-up males
      boast this is Democracy's birthplace,
let them consider us, the silent stone females,
      faces erased, holding up the roof-beams of our race.

THE NEW ATHENA

If the gods are simply players within mortals
    then it's time to lay down my armor, plumed helmet, spear,
the aegis of my goat-skinned shield with gorgon's head.
    I pit difference between peoples: the Egyptians, the Turks,
the Trojans, the States, igniting their battle cry,
    the gore glory of war. Now I must allow my wise side
to emerge from within you, to break the cycle, to calm
    my blood-thirsty brother. I'll have a quiet word
in the ear of Ares. Even he's weary. I must be the deity
    within you who seeks an answer in conflict
without bloodshed, guardian of the small few who command
    with their stentorian voice "No more".

                        Fragment from the lost poem *Athena*
                        The Greek Anthology, Book XVII
                                Adrienne

DISARMING

A middle-aged woman—plain you might say—strolls by
      our house. I was out of sorts, not long up,
but her serene smile, without saying a word,
      remarks: "Take in the sun on the lake,
the honeysuckle's pink fingers bursting into yellow flames,
      the traffic for once on North Avenue gone so quiet
you can hear the whirr of the hummingbird's wings
      reversing in midair." On another morning such serenity
would have vexed me, but there is something so natural
      about her demeanor. She doesn't notice me.
Disarmed, I let what bothers me go
      and think since there's no corresponding god
—the pantheon being all tiresome piss and vinegar—
      we must create a new order and call her
Tranquilia, Calmes, or promote Halcyon and tell Aphrodite,
      Ares, Artemis, even Zeus, to move over in the pecking order,
set her smack in the middle, the woman
      who breezes by our house this divine morning.

WONDER OF WONDERS

A girl cries. Her father beats her, convinces her she's dumb.
    She'll land back in that cave of herself again
and again for the rest of her life. Many are like mythical characters
    blindly returning to tackle whatever invisible monsters
brought them down so long ago. Maybe the wonder
    of wonders of being alive—greater even than the lake
like a glittering shield, the leaves turning tangerine,
    bronze, ruby and so infinitely on—is, as yet,
we have not undone our world,
    what with each individual's struggles,
from ruling leader to regular citizen.
    And should we each manage to wrestle
Trauma to the ground and tame him
    there is Thanatos—his natural father—waiting
at the end of it all, the Big-Wig behind all the trouble.
    Time to give ourselves a pat on the back,
thumbs up, for not having blown ourselves sky high.

THE FIRST STORY

The email, telling a friend *we're not too bad considering*
    the state of the world, crosses the Atlantic
with the touch of a key. The leaves of an evergreen blow
    like a shoal of emerald fish returning to the same place.
A cardinal in his glory pecks the feeder.
    The bells of the Angelus ring from St Joseph's,
the Angel of the Lord declares unto Mary. The infant god
    of my childhood is back on earth again, the one
I've ceased to believe in, the lifebelt that keeps believers afloat
    in the storm of being here, issuing tickets
to the hereafter ever since that episode in the garden,
    the tall tale of our banishment concocted by some storyteller
who'd be so flummoxed we've taken it for gospel
    he'd simply say: "Look around you now. Behold, the garden."

ENVOI

MONARCH BUTTERFLY

Another, another and another flutters
through America. I wish
there were a monarch version of *On The Road*
recording each flaglet's psychedelic trip
of endurance, each a watermark of the soul
held to light, antique symbol.
These flames, lighting off wing-veins of coal,
have waited long enough
to wing-sign "Take a leaf
from us, laying ourselves down in a dark wood,
myriads all together, souls not leaving the body
at death, but emerging into life, a single flame
blazing up from our teeming underworld. Emerge
from your furled chrysalis, become
us all, become the humonarch."

About the Author

Greg Delanty was born in Cork City, Ireland, in 1958 and lived in Cork until 1986. For three months of each year he returns to his Irish home in Derrynane, County Kerry. His most recent books are *The New Citizen Army, The Ship of Birth* (Louisiana State University Press 2006), T*he Blind Stitch* (LSU Press, 2003) and *The Hellbox* (Oxford University Press 1998)). His *Collected Poems 1986-2006* is out from the Oxford *Poets* series of Carcanet Press. He edited, with the scholar Michael Matto, *The Word Exchange, Anglo-Saxon Poems in Translation* (WW Norton, November, 2010). He has received many awards, most recently a Guggenheim for poetry. The magazine *Agenda* has devoted a recent issue to celebrate Greg Delanty's 50th birthday. The National Library of Ireland have recently acquired his papers up to the end of 2012. He is the Past President of the Association of Literary scholars, Critics and Writers. He is a US citizen and an Irish Citizen and teaches at Saint Michael's College, Vermont. He has lived in Vermont since 1986.

Fomite
Burlington, Vermont

Fomite is a literary press whose authors and artists explore the human condition—political, cultural, personal and historical—in poetry and prose.

A fomite is a medium capable of transmitting infectious organisms from one individual to another.

"The activity of art is based on the capacity of people to be infected by the feelings of others." Tolstoy, *What is Art?*

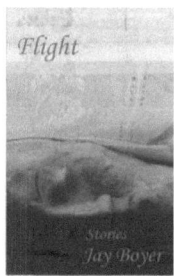

Flight and Other Stories - Jay Boyer
In *Flight and Other Stories,* we're with the fattest woman on earth as she draws her last breaths and her soul ascends toward its final reward. We meet a divorcee who can fly for no more effort than flapping her arms. We follow a middle-aged butler whose love affair with a young woman leads him first to the mysteries of bondage, and then to the pleasures of malice. Story by story, we set foot into worlds so strange as to seem all but surreal, yet everything feels familiar, each moment rings true. And that's when we recognize we're in the hands of one of America's truly original talents.

AlphaBetaBestiario - Antonello Borra
Animals have always understood that mankind is not fully at home in the world. Bestiaries, hoping to teach, send out warnings. This one, of course, aims at doing the same.

Loisaida - Dan Chodorokoff
Catherine, a young anarchist estranged from her parents and squatting in an abandoned building on New York's Lower East Side is fighting with her boyfriend and conflicted about her work on an underground newspaper. After learning of a developer's plans to demolish a community garden, Catherine builds an alliance with a group of Puerto Rican community activists. Together they confront the confluence of politics, money, and real estate that rule Manhattan. All the while she learns important lessons from her great-grandmother's life in the Yiddish anarchist movement that flourished on the Lower East Side at the turn of the century. In this coming of age story, family saga, and tale of urban politics, Dan Chodorkoff explores the "principle of hope", and examines how memory and imagination inform social change.

Fomite
Burlington, Vermont

Still Time - Michael Cocchiarale

Still Time is a collection of twenty-five short and shorter stories exploring tensions that arise in a variety of contemporary relationships: a young boy must deal with the wrath of his out-of-work father; a woman runs into a man twenty years after an awkward sexual encounter; a wife, unable to conceive, imagines her own murder, as well as the reaction of her emotionally distant husband; a soon-to-be tenured English professor tries to come to terms with her husband's shocking return to the religion of his youth; an assembly line worker, married for thirty years, discovers the surprising secret life of his recently hospitalized wife. Whether a few hundred or a few thousand words, these and other stories in the collection depict characters at moments of deep crisis. Some feel powerless, overwhelmed—unable to do much to change the course of their lives. Others rise to the occasion and, for better or for worse, say or do the thing that might transform them for good. Even in stories with the most troubling of endings, there remains the possibility of redemption. For each of the characters, there is still time.

✦ ✦ ✦

Improvisational Arguments - Anna Faktorovich
Improvisational Arguments is written in free verse to capture the essence of modern problems and triumphs. The poems clearly relate short, frequently humorous and occasionally tragic, stories about travels to exotic and unusual places, fantastic realms, abnormal jobs, artistic innovations, political objections, and misadventures with love.

✦ ✦ ✦

The Listener Aspires to the Condition of Music - Barry Goldensohn
"I know of no other selected poems that selects on one theme, but this one does, charting Goldensohn's career-long attraction to music's performance, consolations and its august, thrilling, scary and clownish charms. Does all art aspire to the condition of music as Pater claimed, exhaling in a swoon toward that one class act? Goldensohn is more aware than the late 19th century of the overtones of such breathing: his poems thoroughly round out those overtones in a poet's lifetime of listening."
John Peck, poet, editor, Fellow of the American Academy of Rome

Fomite
Burlington, Vermont

When You Remember Deir Yassin - R.L Green

When You Remember Deir Yassin is a collection of poems by R. L. Green, an American Jewish writer, on the subject of the occupation and destruction of Palestine. Green comments: "Outspoken Jewish critics of Israeli crimes against humanity have, strangely, been called "anti-Semitic" as well as the hilariously illogical epithet "self-hating Jews." As a Jewish critic of the Israeli government, I have come to accept these accusations as a stamp of approval and a badge of honor, signifying my own fealty to a central element of Jewish identity and ethics: one must be a lover of truth and a friend to the oppressed, and stand with the victims of tyranny, not with the tyrants, despite tribal loyalty or self-advancement. These poems were written as expressions of outrage, and of grief, and to encourage my sisters and brothers of every cultural or national grouping to speak out against injustice, to try to save Palestine, and in so doing, to reclaim for myself my own place as part of the Jewish people." The poems are offered in the original English with Arabic and Hebrew translations accompanying each poem.

The Co-Conspirator's Tale - Ron Jacobs

There's a place where love and mistrust are never at peace; where duplicity and deceit are the universal currency. *The Co-Conspirator's Tale* takes place within this nebulous firmament. There are crimes committed by the police in the name of the law. Excess in the name of revolution. The combination leaves death in its wake and the survivors struggling to find justice in a San Francisco Bay Area noir by the author of the underground classic *The Way the Wind Blew: A History of the Weather Underground* and the novel *Short Order Frame Up*.

Roadworthy Creature, Roadworthy Craft - Kate Magill

Words fail but the voice struggles on. The culmination of a decade's worth of performance poetry, *Roadworthy Creature, Roadworthy Craft* is Kate Magill's first full-length publication. In lines that are sinewy yet delicate, Magill's poems explore the terrain where idea and action meet, where bodies and words commingle to form a strange new flesh, a breathing text, an "I" that spirals outward from itself.

Fomite
Burlington, Vermont

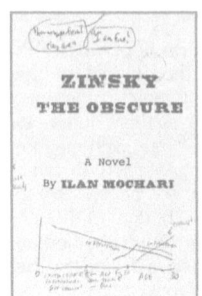

Zinsky the Obscure - Ilan Mochari

"If your childhood is brutal, your adulthood becomes a daily attempt to recover: a quest for ecstasy and stability in recompense for their early absence." So states the 30-year-old Ariel Zinsky, whose bachelor-like lifestyle belies the torturous youth he is still coming to grips with. As a boy, he struggles with the beatings themselves; as a grownup, he struggles with the world's indifference to them. *Zinsky the Obscure* is his life story, a humorous chronicle of his search for a redemptive ecstasy through sex, an entrepreneurial sports obsession, and finally, the cathartic exercise of writing it all down. Fervently recounting both the comic delights and the frightening horrors of a life in which he feels – always – that he is not like all the rest, Zinsky survives the worst and relishes the best with idiosyncratic style, as his heartbreak turns into self-awareness and his suicidal ideation into self-regard. A vivid evocation of the all-consuming nature of lust and ambition – and the forces that drive them – *Zinsky the Obscure* is a novel of extraordinary zeal, range, and power.

The Derivation of Cowboys & Indians - Joseph D. Reich

The Derivation of Cowboys & Indians represents a profound journey, a breakdown of The American Dream from a social, cultural, historical, and spiritual point of view. Reich examines in concise!detail the loss of the collective unconscious, commenting on our!contemporary postmodern culture with its self-interested excesses, on where and how things all go wrong, and how social/political practice rarely meets its original proclamations and promises. Reich's surreal and self-effacing satire brings this troubling message home. *The Derivations of Cowboys & Indians* is a desperate search and struggle for America's literal, symbolic, and spiritual home.

Kasper Planet: Comix and Tragix - Peter Schumann

The British call him Punch, the Italians, Pulchinello, the Russians, Petruchka, the Native Americans, Coyote. These are the figures we may know. But every culture that worships authority will breed a Punch-like, anti-authoritan resister. Yin and yang—it has to happen. The Germans call him Kasper. Truth-telling and serious pranking are dangerous professions when going up against power. Bradley Manning sits naked in solitary; Julian Assange is pursued by Interpol, Obama's Department of Justice, and Amazon.com. But—in contrast to merely human faces—masks and theater can often slip through the bars. Consider our American Kaspers: Charlie Chaplin, Woody Guthrie, Abby Hoffman, the Yes Men—theater people all, utilizing various forms to seed critique. Their profiles and tactics have evolved along with those of their enemies.Who are the bad guys that call forth the Kaspers? Over the last half century, with his Bread & Puppet Theater, Peter Schumann has been tireless in naming them, excoriating them with Kasperdom....
from Marc Estrin's Foreword to Planet Kasper

Fomite
Burlington, Vermont

Views Cost Extra - L.E. Smith

Views that inspire, that calm, or that terrify – all come at some cost to the viewer. In *Views Cost Extra* you will find a New Jersey high school preppy who wants to inhabit the "perfect" cowboy movie, a rural mailman disgusted with the residents of his town who wants to live with the penguins, an ailing screen writer who strikes a deal with Johnny Cash to reverse an old man's failures, an old man who ponders a young man's suicide attempt, a one-armed blind blues singer who wants to reunite with the car that took her arm on the assembly line—and more. These stories suggest that we must pay something to live even ordinary lives.

The Empty Notebook Interrogates Itself - Susan Thomas

The Empty Notebook began its life as a very literal metaphor for a few weeks of what the poet thought was writer's block, but was really the struggle of an eccentric persona to take over her working life. It won. And for the next three years everything she wrote came to her in the voice of the Empty Notebook, who, as the notebook began to fill itself, became rather opinionated, changed gender, alternately acted as bully and victim, had many bizarre adventures in exotic locales and developed a somewhat politically-incorrect attitude. It then began to steal the voices and forms of other poets and tried to immortalize itself in various poetry reviews. It is now thrilled to collect itself in one slim volume.

My God, What Have We Done? - Susan Weiss

In a world afflicted with war, toxicity, and hunger, does what we do in our private lives really matter? Fifty years after the creation of the atomic bomb at Los Alamos, newlyweds Pauline and Clifford visit that once-secret city on their honeymoon, compelled by Pauline's fascination with Oppenheimer, the soulful scientist. The two stories emerging from this visit reverberate back and forth between the loneliness of a new mother at home in Boston and the isolation of an entire community dedicated to the development of the bomb. While Pauline struggles with unforeseen challenges of family life, Oppenheimer and his crew reckon with forces beyond all imagining.

Finally the years of frantic research on the bomb culminate in a stunning test explosion that echoes a rupture in the couple's marriage. Against the backdrop of a civilization that's out of control, Pauline begins to understand the complex, potentially explosive physics of personal relationships.

At once funny and dead serious, *My God, What Have We Done?* sifts through the ruins left by the bomb in search of a more worthy human achievement.

www.ingramcontent.com/pod-product-compliance
Lightning Source LLC
Chambersburg PA
CBHW060342080526
44584CB00013B/876